Scaffolding

Scaffolding

poems by

Peri Best

Sacred Signs Publishing
Box 2903
Grand Forks BC
Canada
V0H 1H0
bestperi@yahoo.com

Sacred Signs Publishing
Box 2903
Grand Forks BC
Canada
V0H 1H0
bestperi@yahoo.com

Front cover design by Gary Tonge
Interior design by Duane Johnson
Illustrations by Peri Best

ISBN 978-1-7389601-0-1 (paperback)
ISBN 978-1-7389601-1-8 (ebook)

First printing: July 2023

With grateful thanks to all you angels out there
Keep up the good work

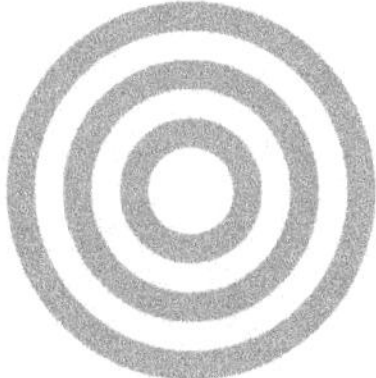

"Love is the outworking of the divine and inner urge
of life."

—Jesus, *The Urantia Book*, 174:1.5

Contents

Preface

Language, both spoken and written, has the power to change how we humans feel and think. The 'coo' and 'no' are our first orientations to life; the one cuddles us closer and the other stops us in our tracks. Words are made of emotional vowels and rational consonants, and together they shape experience. They have certainly shaped mine.

My father claimed I said the word "microphone" at the age of 11 months. Having had children of my own, I highly doubt it. Yet the myth remains. One of my first poems was "Princess Alice" written in Grade Two. Looking back at it, I can see a certain sauciness that is evident in many of the poems I write today.

> Princess Alice is sick in the palace
> Her fever's a hundred and two
> If you go in there and never come out again
> You'll know what happened to you
>
> Princess Alice is sick in the palace
> The doctors are coming by twos
> They're working on her toes
> And they're working on her nose
> And soon they'll be working on her CLOTHES

I fell in love with Shakespeare when I played Viola, the lead in "Twelfth Night," at 17. I discovered that the words of the bard expressed exactly the emotion the actor needed to embody; all one had to do was feel them completely and allow them to resonate throughout the mind and body. Such a powerful experience for both performer and audience! Shakespeare's words, along with my wonderful acting teacher Powys Thomas, taught me to speak, to act and eventually, to write.

Rumi was my next major influencer. Shakespeare's words enlightened the world of human emotional experience, and now Rumi enlightened the world of spiritual experience. Our practice of "the turn" (the whirling dance of the Mevlevi Sufis) involved sitting in a freezing hall at 6:30 in the morning and listening to readings from Rumi's *Mathnawi* (his collected poetical writings in the original translation from Nicholson–sometimes very dry as opposed to the more moving works of Coleman Barks) before we could actually get on our feet. With Rumi, God became something exciting to experience now, not just an Old Testament judge and executioner.

Next in my line of powerful influences is *The Urantia Book*. This astonishing revelation exhibits a power with words that is literally "out of this world." Once the meaning comes clear, truth itself shines out of the black and white shapes on the page. I feel in these many words the simplicity of God's yearning for me. This love shows me what I am, what I can be.

Ideas and imagery interest me. In this collection, I am exploring ways of understanding things like revelation, the soul, our relation to time, the shape of the universe, and how our cosmic parents reveal themselves to us. There is much humor, and I don't say things right out. I hope the levels and patterns will speak to your God spark within.

Poetry was never something I actually focused on; it just happened. It still does. I wake up with an idea or an image, and it rattles around until the beginning words hook me enough to get me to write them down. The rest usually flow out on their own, like they knew what they were doing right from the start.

Words have power, as I started out saying. The power I pray my words will have is for you to "see" something new, experience an understanding "ah ha," be drawn to laugh or remember— even remember something you never knew before. I would take you to another life, a next life, an inner life, your true life. Would that these words would have this power.

May 24, 2023
Grand Forks BC Canada

Rings and Things

Deep in the rose
Abides Her reason for being
A Rose

Not for thorns or roots
Stem or leaves
Or even the purpling petal
But for Beauty
Whose Perfume
Is Perfection

Who can strut
In fashion statement shoes
And hunger after rings
And things that go fast
Who can also know
The Rose
Who emanates from within

See here
Resting in my palm
A petal

Sniff

Gabriel's Song

Mrs. Corey lifts the ladder
And from the moon she sees us spin
Perched on the edge of the Sea of Tranquility
She clicks her heels and giggles with glee
To see the forests disappear in patches
As though a blind man is shaving his beard
Then she rubs her hands with a sound like sandpaper
To see the seas being sifted of life

Who are these greedy guts munching up the world
Not me says the housewife
Not me says the millworker
Not me says the stockbroker
Why we don't use hardly anything at all
Why we have barely enough to get by
It must be THEM
Those other guys
Who tear up the trees
And dredge the oceans
Flattening the hidden water valleys
Where the fish and squidlets play

Mrs. Corey just laughs
She doesn't have to do anything but watch
While the delicious beauty of this world
Is all gobbled up
HA HA HA HA HA

The seedy old lady laughs so hard
She falls off the moon
And lands smack dab
Surprised and aghast
In the golden arms of Gabriel
Angel of beginnings and ends

Who glowers and says
Well now missy
Isn't it about time you got yours

Then a little girl in a striped purple shirt and yellow jeans
Rides up on an old pinto pony

She slides from his bare back and says to Gabriel
I saw you grab this black old crow from the sky
And now you hold her in your arms like a baby
Would you be so kind as to set her down please
Gabriel gladly obliges
And when the scowling brittle old dame
Is propped back up on her old black boots
The little girl marches up to her and says
You can't go on using us like this
For your sport
For your jollies
For your amusement
Don't you know
We are all your family
Who was it cut your feeling cord
The string that ties your heart and your head together
Who left you out in the rain to rust
So now all you do is squeak like an old gate
And call it fun

And when the little girl in the striped shirt steps even closer
Her nose to Mrs. Corey's
Her toes to Mrs.Corey's
The old lady's eyes grow wide with terror
Because when the girl is so close like this
Mrs. Corey can smell on her
The scent of horses and sunshine
Apples and trees
Home made soup

And bare feet running through grass
And it makes her remember

Mrs.Corey turns to Gabriel
Make her stop she whimpers
I am remembering how it feels to be good
And it breaks my mask
Who will I be if I am not who I have been

Then Gabriel lifts his arms
And suddenly
The bit of blue you see between the two
Dissolves
Into one hissing flame

And then it grows dim and ordinary again
And a woman stand there
Not old
Not young
Just a person
Like any person you wouldn't notice on the street

And though this woman lives every day
Holding the idea of her pinto pony close to her hope
Some days Mrs.Corey looks out through her eyes instead
And she scoffs at the world as though it isn't worth saving
And anyone who thinks they can do anything
Is just a stoopeedoo

And when the heavy hopeless weight of Mrs. Corey
Makes the woman feel like giving up
The strong silent voice of Gabriel
Sings this sweet song in her heart
You can do it
I know you can do it
Try

Rags to Riches

Love limps through this world
A beggar bereft
Dragging a shopping cart
Crammed with cast offs
Worn and mostly ruined things
She hopes might have some use in them yet

Love wanders
Unable to find a place to stop
To rest
Until a glimmer
High on a mountain top fogged with smoke
Catches her eye

Suddenly
She is lifted
From the ditch where she crouches
Into a Budget rent a van
And slides up a serpent road
To a pinnacle of luxury
Planted at the top

A gaggle of lovers flock around
Strip her of her rags
Then swathed in silky shiny robes
She twirls in amazement

They ooh and aah together
Then burst into a vast laugh
And all the suffering of the past
Is suddenly naught but a bad joke
Pain drains away
To become the compost of compassion
That is all it ever really is
Right?

Birdie Whispers

When the door to joy seems locked
And you can't even find the street
And the only doors that appear
In the long dark hallway of your life
All seem to open on despair

And even when a little bird of freedom
Lands on your shoulder
And whispers secret directions
To the banquet hall

You keep on walking in your torment
Complaining to the bird
How dark it is

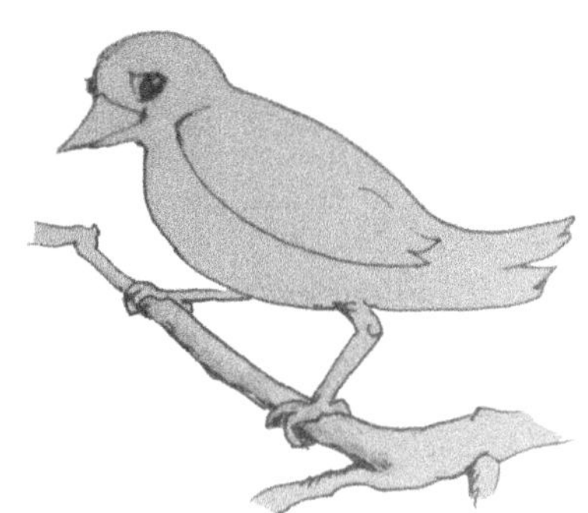

Mantles Within Mantles

For the sake of those who hunger
I draw my mantle close
And here I hold my lover
His cloak enfolds me too

He opens the front of his robe a crack
And from within the folds
Peek the secretly joyous faces
Of all who love as he does

For the sake of those who thirst
I pour out mother's stillness
She is the air
The ground
The substance of everything
Wrapped around him
Wrapped around us

Every atom of her vast body
Dances
Tiny twisting spirals
Like giggles in motion

What's Left

The show must go on
This adage
Is embedded in my theatrical soul
And even though I know
That love
Uncorrupted and pure
Abides
It seems so plastered with the grease paint
Of ages past and present
That it's hard to say
If it's even there at all

I see love walk this world in many guises
Hiding in hearts smothered in shame
Racked by guilt
Compromised by fear and frustration

Let's pretend
The show is over
So
In the dressing room
In front of the mirror surrounded by dazzling lights
I begin

Fearing to see the flaws the makeup
Tried to hide
I scrape off the paint
Peal off the mask
And see only

What's left

Cat Humours

The face of my cat is mottled
Light patches of tan border black
White is where the burning was
She bears witness to cat wisdom
Compiled from all cats gone before
Her coat of many colours
Testifies to her mass of experience

Her direct gaze reflects to me
My own knowing
My body is also a testament
To a pretty rough ride through time

Every single collision of sperm and egg
Preserves some tidbit
Of survival information tossed on
The compost pile of embedded memory
Separate bits
Ultimately settle into
Human humus
Sacred soil
Embraces an even more sacred seed

Whether it was always there
Abiding
Or drawn by need and propitious circumstance
The little god seed quickens into germination
And communion begins

Feathery fine roots reach
To take in nutrients
Squeezed from the cream of ages past
And soon the seed of an immortal soul

Reaches up
In defiance
Of the gravity of this and all other worlds

The seedling soul doesn't even know
It is choosing to grow
Until it breaches the surface of this womb of earth
Where light reveals
Others
Waving away.

My cat winks

Ironing Board

My grandmother would iron her sheets
Until not a wrinkle would interrupt
A vast smooth whiteness

No one seems to iron much anymore
I certainly don't

How can I know I exist
Without the steam of loving eyes
To penetrate the fabric of my being
Release the tension of uncertainty and loneliness
Crumpled up in there
And say
There you are
I see you
You are real

That's what lovers do
We make each other real
We dance
Like exploding water droplets
Straining to hold an infinity of bursting love
Between sheet and board

What if
The love of all the lovers
And carers
And hopers
And prayers
Were melded together as a solid surface
Like an ironing board
And the thin sheet of human inhumanity
Stretched across it and squeezed
By the hot iron of love pressing from above
And so straighten out all the wrinkles

Pssssshhht

The Body of a Universe

Look at what we have here
A tome
A great big Holy Tome
Called holy
Because for the longest time
This was all that remained
Of a once bountiful body of living truth

Strained through the sieve of time
These precious morsels
Painstakingly preserved
Have become shrivelled and curled
Hardly recognizable
As parts of a once vibrant creation

Suddenly
Appearing as out of a troubled sky
A waterfall rains down
To reconstitute
The bits that might once have been
A brain, a body, a heart, a spirit
And like dried mushrooms that swell with soaking
They now become useful and succulent

This true blue waterfall
Is partitioned into four
As a circular stained glass window
Is divided by a cross

The spiral shape of life is revealed

The past a snake
Bumps in its body evidence
Of only partly digested events

The future of now empties into a growing luminosity
And I look
Again and again fascinated
By the blossoming reality
Of Self

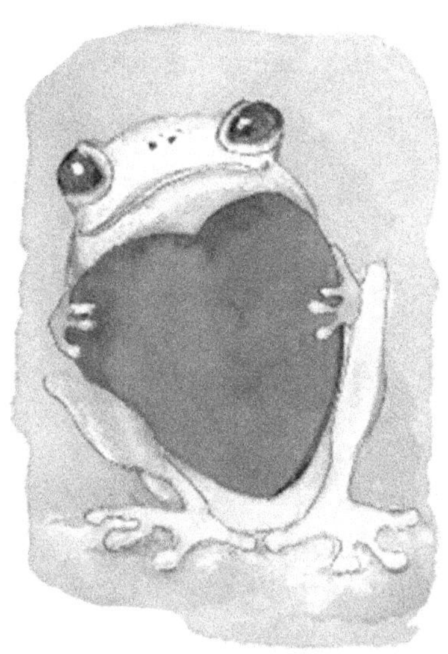

O My Craving Soul

Under a shroud of mourning
A gentle presence
Slips into the seat of my certainty
Like the battery pack for my electric snowblower
Snicks into its housing

This new
Yet strangely familiar entity
Raises a perky head
And like February's groundhog
Gazes around with freshly opened eyes
Certain there's sunshine somewhere

Willing
O so willing
To greet with grace
Each moment of possibility
This fuzzy muppet ever so comfortably
Slips over the hand
Of the Great Operator
Hidden behind the inner curtain

This ambiguously sexed being
Translates myriad and manifold mysteries
Into a message
Easily understood
By all of us unruly two year olds
Running around this mortal playroom.

February 3, 2022 The day after my cat Mimi's passing

Firefly Fusion

Oh oh
Getting dark
That curtain of night drops
Again

Alone
The dark is no comfort
What can I do
What can I do

I crawl
Stretch my wings
And fly blind into shadowy blackness

Feelers extended
Yearning fills me

Something inside bursts
I shine

And there you are
Shining too

His Father's House Has Many Mansions

His death is swept away
Like flattened blue black feathers from beside the freeway
And because he can't stand to smell the popcorn
When he never gets to eat it
He leaps from his pink padded coffin
To see what's beyond

He free falls away from this world
Because the living gravity that sucks things into shapes
Like mountains and eggbeaters
Angora sweaters and mothers
Agrees to let him go
To see if he is willing to make the journey
Through octaves of bettering spheres

His mother waits on the other side and chews her cuticles
Afraid he'll miss the shining diamond
Of hope for love eternal
That sparks so deep and dense beyond despair

He bent and broke so many times and ways
It's hard for her to tell if he will grasp
The proffered hand of seraphic love
And pull himself into the game
Where he might learn to live
Again
Again
Until he has no body apart from theirs
No curiosity
No relative comparisons
No heart to hope or break in
Just One with the Endless Boundless
A Cabalistic Ultimatonic Ain Soph

There
Do you hear that
A sound like a Great Big Gulp
Is it the winking smiling snake
Ever so properly attired in top hat and tail
Admitting his end into his own beginning

What will it be boyo
A crap shoot
Double or nothing

Snake eyes

Love Gets Around

Astride my merry-go-round horse of glittery magnificence
I bounce toward winter

Gears underneath
Invisible to me up here on my trusty steed
Turn and mesh with other gears
Smaller and larger

We all turn together
Autumn to winter
This year to next
This sun around a distant nebula

And all of us
ALL
Turn around the non-dimensional point
Of No Movement At All!

Mirrors often hide this center
But we know it's there
Don't we

We who ride this carousel
Clutch the pole for stability
Wave our plastic cowboy hats
And grin out at Mom and Dad

Suddenly She Slipped

Suddenly she slipped
Through the skin of time
And was caught floating
With apparent abandon
In the bloodstream of God

Subsumed in warm bumping red promise
She has no more need for belief
For faith
For judgement
For comparisons
All are drowned
In Being
Now

She slipped out of Time
As she knew it
And into Existence
As it is
Just a corpuscle
Changing colour
On her way to the heart of it all

One Nest

Revelation
Appears today as a broody hen
Who lowers her fluffy bottom
Snuggling all eggs in her nest
Alike

Although some of her eggs
Are a little off white
The potential clutched within
Grows
The same
Or not

Some think brown eggs are best
My Banty hens laid green and blue ones
But the truths of warmth and time
Hatch a living line of golden light
Connected through hens to the source
Of all suns just the same

Eggs grow
And as a sidebar
Nourish us

Clear plasm surrounds
A yellow circle
The white is bound by shell in an ovoid
Together they presage a new revelation
Destined to burst

Miniature rainbows reflect off her feathers
As a glint of sunlight
Finds her snuggled in the shadows

One light
Many colours
One hen
To bind them all

A Surfeit of Perfection

Some of us are like the earth
We feel the weight
Of everyone who sparks into being

We could not be separate
If we shut off all our senses
And knew nothing but the beating
Of the heart that holds the blood
Of all the mothers and fathers
Sisters and brothers
Forever before
Forever after

All lives beat in us
Like hearts
Like drums

My faith grows or stagnates
At the centre of the garden of self
No one chooses for another
Whether the finger in the dam
Holds the living water in
Or out

Whose voice is it that cries
I am drowning in you God
And seeks to be saved

Who is so smothered
In a surfeit of perfection
That she will seek surcease
Of truth and light and joy so overpowering
That goodness cannot contain it

Fried Desire

Frying in my own juices
It's hotter and crisper than stewing
This juice just won't mix
With the oil of objective reality
It pops unexpectedly
And burns my face

Someday the turned on taps of my fortune
Will overflow into the stream of destiny
And carry this raft
Right over the horizon into the future
And there
On that bright Judgement Day
Crowned in glory
My hand will be reached for
By the realer than a ghost of a true love
Who will leap from the bushes
Where he has been hiding all along
And he will cover my eyes with fragrant hands and whisper
Guess who
And I will know
And the weight of wasted years of wanting
Will fall from my hips
Where it has been hiding my overwhelming joy
So long and heavy

O what sweet relief it will be
To see this lumpy old skin
Suddenly puddle there on the ground
Where some kid will find it
And stoop to peek
Gingerly lifting the edge
With only fingernails

Expecting perhaps
Some new born monster to slither out
Never guessing that the beauty of butter has flown

If I weren't a woman
Would I feel like this

Did Jesus too
Long for the love of his life
Or was he bright enough to realize
For certain
That he already had her

Dreams don't care
If the dream
Is fruit of days of passion spent
Or seeds of joy to come
They burn
Unattended
Clutched close as a candle
In the hands of a desperate caroller
Singing
O Holy Night
O Night Divine
And
Long lay the World
Like all of us over the hill ladies
Who linger in pale confusion
Amid the detritus of a life half lived
The word Accomplishment
Reflecting the unspent ammunition
In the arsenal of our desire

Many Wombs

Out of the paradox
That is Man and Woman
A vortex of new life is drawn

Soft and warm
The first womb grows a form
In which choices will be made

Who I is
Is learned in the second womb
Whose walls are the many arms of family

A just begun self
Reflects all influences
Leaves no cone unturned
For every seed feeds the formation
Of values and disappointments
Each need fed
Spawns a new one
Milk to motorcycles
Slinkys to sex

Insidious as ooze
Society squeezes the flimsy structure of a home
And spits a fledgling identity into the third womb

Baby suddenly turns to scream
At the Mommy face
At the Daddy face
Hanging there in the mirror
And from the acned visage
There spews forth
Blame

Why didn't you prepare me
For this

It takes a heck of a lot more than luck
To end up with any sympathetic people after this birth
Yet some do seem to slide right out
Caesarian sectioned almost
Greased by slippery old lucre
They plop into the ready-made bassinet
Of a law firm
Or a diplomatic appointment

The fourth womb births an itty bitty cheeping human soul
With or Without
A human body

Each womb seems to hold endless possibility
At first
But becomes cloying and tight fitting
As need grows
This is how we know we are about to be born
The world we are in becomes stale and understandable
Time a whip of duty and obligation

We kick against the mushy red walls
And buy a new corvette
Fanaticize about food
Get a facelift
We try to turn back
But our heads get stuck
And crooked and twisted
We myopically grasp
For the distracting passion
That used to be the curse of the divorce courts
And now wish we could rub back into flame

This is the longest labor yet
And if we don't believe that the angels are waiting
With rubber gloves outstretched
To catch us when we drop
From the body of human culture
As we have grown to know and hate it
We will hang on the edge
Clinging to the long hairs of her dickey-die-doe
And rationalize
Philosophize
Pontificate
Berate
And generally resist getting on with it

The eager eyes of the angels whisper
"Come on little god
Come out and play
Here's your whole new universe
We've painted it a fresh true blue
Just for you
Just for you"

Precious

Spring loaded
The screen door slams
Dusty boots clomp to the sink
Water sluices over grimy blood caked hands
Which in turn
Splash then hold
A care lined and wind baked face
A deep breath
Held
Then slowly sighed away

It's not as though death is something new
You'd think after all these years out here
He'd be used to it
But she'd been just about to pop
The other ewes hadn't a scratch on 'em
It was the nice one
The one that would come up and ask for a pet
The one who'd been bottle fed
Might'a known

Must of been that dog
He'd seen it a few times scrounging around
Hate shooting dogs
Hate shooting anything
But what else you gonna do

Might of been a coyote
But with the river so high
It was hardly likely they'd of found their way over

Must of been that dog
The folks across the way had just got it for their kids

Who gets a German Shepard for kids
Hate shooting dogs

Poor Precious
The ewe'd had her neck ripped open
Then a huge chunk just chewed from her back end
Must of been last night
When he was out at that silly meeting
He'd had a feeling not to go
But then the Calverts came over and offered to drive him
Couldn't very well say no

The phone rang
It was that new lady down the road
An artist they said
Couldn't be doin' too much art
Cause every time he went past her place
She was out doin' something with her horses
Or the fence
Or the garden
Rain or shine

Seems she had a couple of sheep too
One'd had an ear ripped open
And a chewed up leg
Did he know what might of done it
Well yeah probly

He told her about Precious
She sounded genuinely sorry
They agreed the most likely culprit was the dog
And that someone needed to confront the folks
She offered to go
He wasn't much on telling people
That their kid's dog had to be killed

There didn't seem like there was must more to say
But he didn't want to hang up
Today he just wanted to feel some connection to life
To hope
To any kind of reason to go on
And she was there
It got too much some days
Being alone all the time
And it seemed he'd been holding death
A lot more often than life
Recently

She might 'av heard something of his need in his silence
She didn't chatter like most women
She was there
Just there
Breath joined by wire
Their thoughts and feelings
Ephemeral at the best of times
Seeped along the strand
To the tune of unspoken hope
And ghost songs of antique affairs

Poor Precious
Precious days
Precious moments
The reaper doesn't wait
His rhythm relentless
When his sharp scythe slices this thin connection
Summer skies and strawberries
Breakfast and horse breath
Slippery bodies and sparkling eyes

What next

Whatever

They hold each other
Close to their ears
And breathe

She diffidently asks
Would he be interested in dinner sometime
Just as diffidently he says
Sure
Frozen food can get awfully boring
Day after day

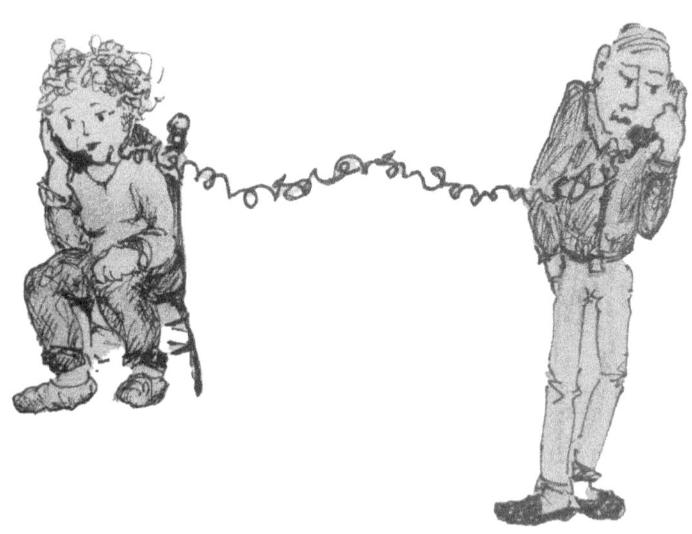

The Future of Death

So Adam says to Eve
What can we do to make this right?
Our blood was meant to cool the hormonal fire
That tears their lusting lives apart
Hormones that still tend to rule
In spite of the adjusting essence
Clamouring
For true love to circulate in there
Instead

What can we do
To keep them
From diving off bridges
Head first into traffic
To let them know
That stitched into their hearts
Are wings
That will grow
If only they choose
To stretch them

Now that death cannot catch us up
In the defeat and despair it once did there
And since our parents demand
We patch up the wounds
Clean up the mess
What else can we do?
Our legions of willing angels
Are here to offer sweet nudges
But they are so often dismissed
As foolish sentiment or fantasy

Perhaps we'll hold our linked hands up

And invite them to play
London Bridges with us
And as they pass through our invisible portal
They'll be caught up in the dance
The aspiralling circle dance
We all learn together
How to place the feet
Just here
How to hold the hand
Just so

Just so
The perfect match is made
Making a match
With not a hint of sulphur
Just

Music
And the spark of
Fusion

Zipper

Now you see it
Now you don't
Here you are
And now you're not

Positive space/ negative space
Existence shows itself
As a two headed monster
With no point of orgasmic intersection
Until
Bodies equipped with complementary bits
Join at the bottom
And slickly matching tooth to space
Zip up

Some never get started
Skewed at the beginning
The slider won't rise
And if the zips are of different gauges
There's no chance of ever getting closure

Only choosing the path of synchrony
Allows for ascent

Some get stuck somewhere in the middle
Leaving top and bottom
To flap unconnected

Most zippers
Have little awareness
Of the world of sweater
They are responsible for bringing together

They only care about the bit of thread
Binding them to the fabric
Clinging
Not realizing what they cling for

The will to connect
To ascend in concert
Is dependent on the power of the slider
To bring them into alignment
And keep them there

As they approach the top
Vague gurgles and mutterings
From the throat nearby
Intimate inklings of purpose
And reasons for it all

Holding a world
Of intermeshed threads together
Is a sacred calling

Some joiners are simple buttons
Some toggles
Or snaps
Some just cling and weave as they are able
But the joining journey of the zipper
Ah
That's something to aspire to

Sigh

Note: A Canadian invented the zipper

Cedar

My mother is a cedar tree
The moist earth of heaven
Nourishes her every fibre of beingness
Here

Shifting motes of light
We be
We be
We sing and suffer
And she sifts our lives
With her lacy fingertips

In her core
His living presence hides
And from there
The love they make
Echoes in the many branched chorus
Of exuberant angels
Whispering their urgent invitation
To join
To join
To come and join
Us

We'll sit
And dance
Breathe
And feast
Beneath a beaming sky

UPW of G

We fold the gift
Of this fresh moment
Like origami
Into the postal station
Of Everliving Mind

We
The Untied Postal Workers of God
And I
Sort and select tidbits of time tested truth
To be copied
Dispersed
And flung about a waiting universe

I caught a thought
Of enlightened and enwisened joy
Shot straight from Arcturus
And here
Now
I give it to you

For those of you who think
That life ends with the evening news
And begins with a new hairdo
We post this announcement

Spark

Someone in Switzerland sourced my DNA
Specifying in a very general way
The lands of my ancestors

My links to many people spiderweb into the past
I know for sure I have been
But not who or that I will be

Unless

I earn my real name

When

A spark
Between the fingertips
Of two hands
One hand the stuff of being
The other
The stuff of possibility
Illuminates me
Annihilates me

Poof goes the fusion
And then
My name tag firmly affixed to my chest
I'll be on my way to Being
A gleam in the eye
Of the Big Giant Head

Who is not a snake with its tail in its mouth
But a curious face
Waiting to see the sparks fly

Up Up Up

Swing low
Drop into my attic
Hook me and pull me
Up up up

Bring as much of me
As the rope will hold
Lift me out of this mud sucking darkness

A schlupping wet pop
And I gasp
A whiff of sweet air
Promises light

From up here
I look down
Where unloved body parts
Linger
Lost in a confusion of desires

I set my sights to swing on a star
And slingshot
Into the bullseye
At the centre of
Blue concentric rings

Once there
I will bounce back
To drop my hook
Into the morass
And lift you
Up
Up

Up

No Bounds

Only in my mind
No longer in my body
Does that deep and penetrating passion burn

Who I am
Is not who I was
At least chemically

Maybe I am not through with love
But maybe I am
What now

Do I
Like Elizabeth
The Virgin Queen
Marry my world
Live only for the moments
When I spread instead
My fingers
And explode a healing balm over all

Sh baby sh
Your mother is busy loving too much
So I will Grandmother you
And since my love
Now knows no bounds
Of age or sex or species
I will hold you close
And hum a song
Of peace and serenity
Unbroken by the sobs of the unrequited

I Am Not a Rock

I am
And
I am not
A Rock

To you I may look
Like just one of myriad multi-coloured and diversely shaped
Rocks by the river
But I tell you a secret
I take quiet delight in the flecks of green and red
Black and white that were fired
Into the designs worn into me
Into me and the others nestled around me
By exploding earth and squeezing
By the shifting touch of the ageless river

You might think I am limited by my shape
Forever doomed to isolation by my hard edges
Even though much of the sharpness has been worn off
By the years of tears
Yet still I know what I am
Inside

Common granite
For the most part
Found mostly in mountainous areas
I am part quartz
Oxygen and silicon
Mixed with sodium and potassium feldspar

Oxygen
This I share with the air
Potassium and silicon and the other minerals

With the earth and trees and the deer
Who tip toe over me to get a drink

Look closer
I am a molecule
I am an atom
I spin
And hold the space of universes
In my orbits

I am the most minute bit
Of indivisible matter
Spit from the womb of Infinity
And inside me
Is Paradise

Believe me
I know

I am not
A Rock

If The Moon

If the moon had been able
To push its way past
The streetlights and leaves
I would have seen it
Cast a path of moonbeams

You looked as though
The lack of ants upon the sidewalk
Was a great disaster

On seeing me
You saw me looking
Sparkling in the light
Reflected light of prisms
Bent
Finding in your eyes a mirror

Seated on the pig shorn grass
You told me to tell all
Glimmering
I started

Of shaken waters spewing through me
And feeling slightly ill
As trails of past endeavours
Learned the laws of motion
And moving like a monarch on migration

Mosaics on a railway track
Pretending to be drunks
We wove and sat and caged ourselves
Within the plated glass

Confusion and the ferris wheel
And continually channelled
With fingers in my mouth
Cotton candy sticks

The apes now fought their tribal wars
All females must be saved
You know the way they jump about
Flailing arms and legs

Kill the lights
Reeling round
The murder was arranged
But victims not complying

You know my head the night before
Had boggled in a book
Then it boggled
Back and forth
In and out
A strobe

Then you and now
And more to come

They talked of needles of veins
Of flagging blood
I tried to stop it
But they
They knew what they wanted

My coming in and lying down
Completely clothed in jeans
And feeling very cold

I'd thought of walking in the dew
Make experiences
Chalk it up
But you wanted to make love
So

He came
I cried
I'm talking now to you
And told him
But he said
Don't worry
I love you as you are

The Wren

She sings and sings and sings
A hopeful sounding song

It breaks my heart

Alone
Last wren singing
Her babies torn to bits
By the squirrel
I'm guessing
Since it crouched so possessively
Over the little house
And fought the stick I used
To try and chase it away

She sings and sings
Small and brave
She breaks my heart

All creatures
Who are here to teach us Other-Beingness
Whom we have displaced
Poisoned and hunted
All are yours Mother
And I turn to you now
For hope
For comfort
And
I sing
I sing
I sing

Truth Dog

Truth sneaks up like a stray dog
Who's been lurking in the bushes nearby
Waiting
No telling how long
Alert for the right moment
To make her tentative appearance
Hope simmers in her eyes
Is there a future here?
Is this someone willing to see me?

She's a belly-scraping-on-the-ground hound
Who lifts next to hopeless eyes
Apologizing for her very existence
Fear of rejection
Possibly violent rejection
Clear in every quivering fibre

Truth is not tame or kind or civilized
She's a bitch
And once you've let her in
She demands you pay attention
Now

Even to consider admitting
This walking hunger into one's life
Is to shatter
The fragile pattern already in place

The young seem to find it easier
To toss it all
To make room for this so obviously unloved dog
But the old -
Not so willingly accommodate the inconvenience
Of the mangy cur

Nonetheless
She lingers still
Dangling the possibility of companionable walks
And games of mutual enjoyment

You see
Once you know she's there
Truth is not then so easily banished to the bushes

Besides
There might be beasts there in the shadows
With hungers of their own
Who would tear our Truth to pieces
If ever they caught her scent

Inklings of Love

O look
It's a baaybeee
Soooo soft
Soooo smooth
Little senses like octopus arms
With hungry pulsing suckers seek
A one and a
Two
Makes one and one makes two
But when two make a three
The two must entertain
Those probing tips of need and validation
Or
Faster than egg yolk slipping through fingers
Back into self made inky darkness
The uncharged inkling will dive
There to skulk amidst poisonous anemones

O embrace me in your receptive ionized waters
Cries the one who is learning fear fast
Do not zap me with power surges of anger
Confidence draining critiques
Or cloying honey expectations
I am your own little Frankenstein
Pulling on the stiff switches of your affection
And eating your words and memories
Let a classic song of the bio-electric chemistry between you
Entice me back into your atmosphere

Short-circuited babies
We're still hungry and sparking
Half a century later

Come

Free my people
This is my marching order
I hear it loud and clear

So I learn about oppression
And how to walk the fine line
Between the dark weight of tradition
And the freedom of original thought and creativity

Rankled at the imposition of ignorant authority
I buck and squirm
Until tamed enough
To see how the pitiable embittered souls
Strangle in their Windsor knots

A seeker seeking keys comes
To free me from my chains
Especially the ones
I didn't know I was dragging

Recognition is a most useful key
I see you and know you again
Always for the first time
I feel the encompassing ocean
Sloshing in us all

The older I get
The more keys
I forget I have in my pocket

The intricate skeleton key of music
Unlocks the locks
That hold apart our little boats
Marooned at different levels

And touch
The hint of connection in the reaching fingers
Of God and Adam
On a chapel ceiling
The essence of it all
In the space between their tips

Then words
These words
Sometimes slide into the puzzle mechanism
Where feelings are unknown
Until spoken

I am a victim
A prisoner of this life
This body
Until the taut fingers of the key
Line up with the waiting spaces
In my mind
My heart
And spirit
And turn me

I am now the open door
Come

An Aria To Beauty

Because I know
I am surrounded by beauty
I am full
And death
Has no power
Over me

Beauty
Is the reflection
Of all that sings
Within me

A chorus of light and shadow
Hums behind my eyes
A ghost of a memory
Peaks at me from around the corner
And I am more than now
I am always

So
Shall we sing
And fill the emptiness
With the sparkling fire of sound without fear
For joy has no counterpart
She lives
Even without me
She lives

This Day

This day has left the sky bereft
Of all but a bit of blue
Shreds of cloud
Pulled from the west
Block
What might have been starlight

Music drips from his fingers
Seeps into her ears
Then saunters off
Into the beginning of nightfall

Floods come
The legacy of duning snow
Humans brace against
A siege of tears

In silhouette against the French doors
They pray

The earth wrings her hands

Michael's Day

Sweet red limbs
Curtained by fringes
Of glossy green fingers
Round out a day
Of jagged beginnings

Cut
We bleed
And see in crimson life outpouring
A gasp of meaning
A slash of truth

Tears
Eye pearls
Shimmer
Brimful of sudden slamming insight

Our days are framed
By the legs of lives past and yet to come

Creator Father
Take your bow today
As do I to you

Chain Links

Journeying through this jungle
I come upon a chasm
Far too steep and wide
To cross without some bridge

So to start
I make a sling of string
And lob it across the gulf
Tied to a rock

It keeps falling short
Until I see you there
Waiting to catch it

My thought
Wrapped tight to this rock I toss into the past
Now links us
With the memory of bodies
We are both part of

Eve
My myth
My archetype
My mother
My sister
Your anguish has resounded through us all
Til this promising morning

I hold this thread
And tie it to a chain
And eventually
Pulling stronger and stronger stuff across
It becomes a bridge
And together we cross the chasm of time

We are one and not wrong
The links of this chain
Bind us with shame no longer

55

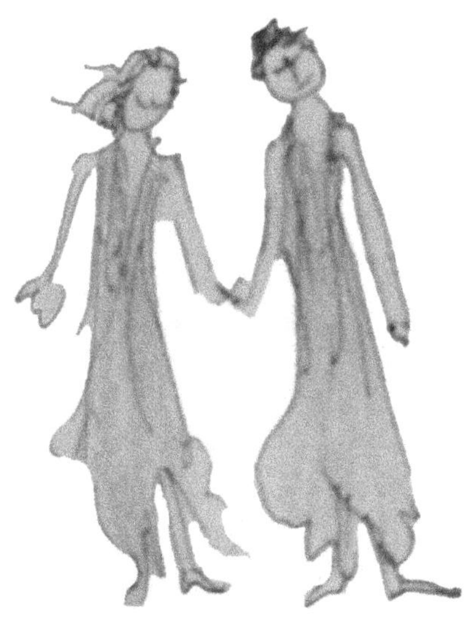

Don't Help Me I'm Falling

Falling into your love
Lord
A sound like terror
Is torn from the base of my being

The winds of our passion
Redolent of pungent earth
And honey laced moisture
Embrace the shape of my passing

How can I fall
So far
When you are
So close

This Christmas

This Christmas let us walk like fearful pages
And step carefully into the larger footprints
Of the great one who strides before us
Both king and vulnerable infant
Ebullient source of all good things
He is Saint Nicholas and a Sinter Klaus
And a jolly coke drinking winker

This Christmas let us not forget
That we all struggle through the same storm
The snow deep
The night cold and long
But if we hold hands and follow the leader
Like the kindergarteners do
We might become soft at the edges
And dare to believe
That Goodness is where we are going
And Love is what melts the snow

Where the Roses Go

On graph paper he charts where the roses go
And once precisely planted
He sprays them when the aphids arrive

He clips a few choice blooms to bring inside
He floats them in a large glass bowl
Then covers it tightly with cellophane
They'll last longer that way
He thinks

Preserved
Unsmellable and distorted by plastic
First one turns brown and slimy
And before he notices
They all do

Then responsibly
He turfs them into the neat compost
Still wondering why his wife left him

The Whole Shebang

My lover like a mighty train
Blew right past my station

I'd been waiting and hoping
But when he finally came
I guess I just didn't wave hard enough
To catch the eye of His Engineer

I am left drawing in the scents of his passing
That whiff of diesel
Iron pressed against iron
More a taste than a smell

And the tracks

I know where he's gone because I can follow his tracks

His Engineer rides up front
The passengers eat and gossip
Sleep and speculate dreamily
As worlds flow by

Then there are those
Eager to have us join in the ride
Who toss out a hook on a line
From the back of the caboose

All I need to do is catch it
And they will reel me in

Perhaps if they squint
They will see the cords of love
Wrapped around me
Connecting me to you
And all the living we've experienced
So when they get me
They get the the whole shebang

Pattern

Pattern is beauty's way of making love
Real

The first idea of love
Elegantly unfolds into the universe
To hit us at the speed of light

Because I need and want
I try to grasp the light
To seek relief from tension and grief and loss
O such loss
I know if I could meet that ultimate challenge
Conquer my fear of loss
I would be
Enlightened
And never have to grasp again

Despite the wrench of grief
I bare my belly to light today
And go to the place
Where light passes through me
To cast
I pray
A pleasing pattern into the world

That's what you want of me
Isn't it
My precious Mystery Monitor
Just let us be beauty
You whisper
And together we shall see
O what sights we shall see

This is our urge to merge and mirror
And together spray love into paisley fractals
The cosmic and the minuscule
The pattern of light
Divine

I Wiped Her Body

When my mother in law died
I wiped her body

Will you wipe my body
Or will I wipe yours

When you take leave
My friend
Will I catch you
As you leap the great abyss

Or will I wipe your body

Dancing Laundry

Barely pinned to the clothesline
Of this existence
She sheds all
But a thin grey blanket
That masks
Or warms perhaps
Her eighty year old hide

The secret smile on her lips
Is the only sign
That visions
Play in her mind
Dance in her heart

Memories of greatness
Faith and solidarity
Keep her feet moving
To follow the officers of the court
As they lead her away

—Ode to a Sons of Freedom woman seen in front of the courthouse in Nelson

Mother of All

I woke
Naked on your breast
You flowed into me and filled me

Though I had eyes
I couldn't see you
You were so big

Fed
I grew
Until your gaze drew me
To see my own reflection there

I shivered awake

I look for you everywhere now
You are small and you are big
Your bounty sustains me still

Lost Babies

Slippery things from the beginning
They worm themselves into any place
They figure you haven't been

Arrogant as all get out
History is no blessing
In their religion of being new
They go places and find trouble enough
To make you crazy for years

How did she find that hole
The camouflaged one
With the baited sharp-toothed trap at the bottom
Perhaps she thought wonderland waited there
White rabbits became instead
White death
A powder coating of make-believe power

O baby
Can my love follow
Where your demented feet have led you
Are you running away from me
Or toward
A dark and grinning gigolo

You want a body that's wanted
Want a wit that charms
You want to wield the heavy cape of magic
And make all dreams come true

The ways of everyone else
Aren't good enough
Aren't the ones to satisfy you

I shine my desperate flashlight
Into the labyrinth
Into the cozy hell you found
I fear to find your broken body
But when I shine the beams into your dilated pupils
I see your mind has been broken instead

Now found and synthesized
And resting in stabilized neural pathways
A newly remade you
Wants to be you again

Together we find a life worth living
In the little things
And you are my baby once more
You smile
You trust
You step into the world
You hold before you the gift of your pain
A pain that is the history of all pain
Being redeemed
All over again

Fits and Starts

The tip of the pole of love
Smacked me last night

I am wavering in the slight vertigo
And my stomach hasn't quite decided
Whether it was the wine
Or the sudden lurch it made
When you said I was beautiful
And you stroked the arm of the couch
As though it was my hair

They say noses
Are indicative of size

The only real question
Is one of fit

What's Left

The show must go on
This adage
Is embedded in my theatrical soul
And even though I know
That love
Uncorrupted and pure
Abides
It seems so plastered with the grease paint
Of ages past and present
That it's hard to say
If it's even there at all

I see love walk this world in many guises
Hiding in hearts smothered in shame
Racked by guilt
Compromised by fear and frustration

Let's pretend
The show is over

In the dressing room
In the mirror surrounded by dazzling lights
I begin to take it off
Fearing to see the flaws that the makeup
So successfully has compensated for
I scrape off the paint
Peal off the mask
And I see only

What's left

Circles of Pi

He draws a circle of endless pi
This is a representation
Not to scale
He says

And what the teacher points to
Is either so much bigger
Or infinitely smaller

Like this picture of the universe I have for you here
Ascending orbits of circles and circuits
That spiral up and out in order to get you from here
In time
To there
In space and even beyond

Zoom in
Zoom out
And see

A foetus floating in its sac in space
A 2001 projection

An explosion
Like cartoon sound waves blown from a megaphone

A massive mother
Breathing the ecstasy
Of her endless orgasm with him

A spec of light
In the blackness of your eye

We think big or small
Conceive of patterns
And see how we are woven into them

It's all a matter of scale
The circle is endlessly
One

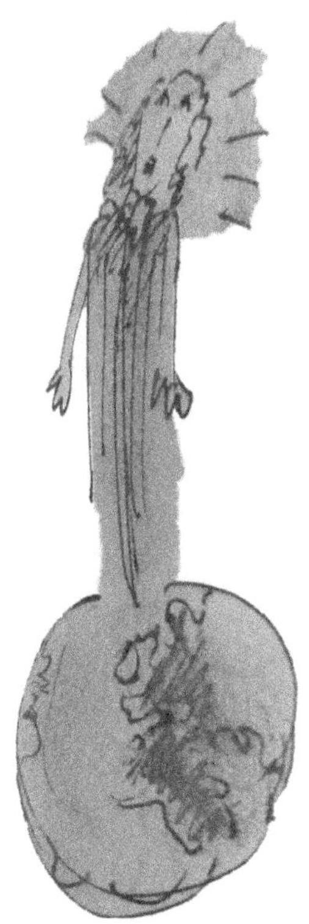

Her Hands

Her hands hold a cigarette
Rothmans
Elegant
Fourth and fifth fingers curl into her wrist

I missed the sight of her hands
Wiping the bums of babies

But I did see her hands
Weaving in desperate supplication
As if strumming the harp
Of her prodigal child's existence

And now
A brush loaded with white paint
Perfects
Over and over
A solemn and defiantly luscious
Cow

Our hands
Together
Shape hope

Essence

Cool barely fresh morning air
Spills through the dam of glass above our heads
Blessing us
With essence of mountain
Ponderosa pine
Mullein
And faint starlight

Percolate

The dregs of dinner
The almost niece and nephew
Off on their global searches
For love

Bits of memory
Are distilled into words
Phrases
I put the salad dressing in the fridge

Old dog chews bones
I hope I don't have to clean it up later

Love leaves traces
No matter how impossible it seems at times
It is still love
And it leaves a ghost of color
A tantalizing scent
A breath of being
Passing

Mything

All is myth
The stories of lives
Ideas and thoughts
Are rooms
For hearts to understand in

We wrap our stories around ourselves
So we can find comfort
Amidst the mystery
Of Being

Windows

It's way too dark in here
Open up the windows
Let's get some light in here

Shuttered
Not just with heavy curtains
That keep out heat or cold
But storm shutters
Put up long ago
So we could weather the terrible tempest
That once ravaged this world

But now it's time
To unfasten the bolts grown rusty with disuse
Grab a can of WD-40 and give 'em a shot

The rust resists
But lo
The wonders of modern technology
Plus mighty determination
Win the day
And the grey boards give way to reveal

A spring day
Abounding with birds and blue and infant green
All is hope

We shove open the next

Winter
Snow and diffuse light
The persistent appearance of death and despair

A screech of hinges
And
Surprise

Autumn leaves
Fill the dense air with a musty warmth
Efforts were made and we live with the harvest

The last one shows

Late summer
A dazzling noonday sky ablaze with seraphim
Wavering in the vastness of forever like a mirage

Earth ears hear only a hint
Of their glorious oratorio as it reverberates throughout
Our universe
Nonetheless all witness
Inexplicable miracle

The source of all light
Glows
In a wee baby boy

His radiance
Dances the spring
Melts the snow
Redeems the fall
And beautifies even the cobwebs in the corners
Of this old house

Scaffolding

Imagine
Vast empty space
You aren't even there

Then
What's that
Waaaay out there
A spot
A dot of
Something
Light

Zoom in
The light glows like an expandable Chinese lantern
When looked at from above
Three concentric circles
Appear like ripples in a pond
Blue shines at the very center
And yellow
Then crystal red radiates around

Motes of the different hues
Joyously rub against each other
Their friction creates sparks
And these children of light
Become the many shapes of being
Unfolding into time
Seven variously hued petals
Surround a vibrating rosy blossom at the core of it all
Its fragrance permeates all space
To remind all the children
What home they come from
And how to get back

When they decide
They want to know again
The loving light of joy that made them

Many down stepping leaps through time and space
In cascades of seven
Bring us to
Here now
You
Us

Your blood has finally learned to circulate
In a being crowned with wisdom
And singing a song of worship prompted praise
It was only dreaming
When the rosehips containing the seeds were dropped
And prodded into germination

Molecules of iron
Squeezed from the marrow
Remember the whole trip
Through trilobites and triceratops
Frogs and lemurs
Circling round and spiralling up
Til it spun itself into
You

Many octaves of colour and time eventuate in you
Here
Wondering
Who you really are
And how you got to be this way

You catch a whiff
The scent of a rose?

And when you do
The bit of blue from that very center
Reaches out and down to you and lands
Right in the middle of your head

From there
This loving blue
Like a parent
Invites you to trust that
He/She/It knows the Way

The Way the perfume of love leads
So you can melt into the Light of the One Rose
Again

Sounds like a pretty much perfect plan
Right
This Way of light and love and a life of roses
Being goes out
Experiences everything
Comes home to share
Then be part of the next outreach
Easy peasy

But
Once upon a time
There was this cocky guy in middle management
Who'd been relegated to a half forgotten corner of the red belt
Who thought he knew
A Better Way
And he got a bunch of other bored bureaucrats
To kick up a riot with him

Perhaps they'd lost the primal blueprint
You know

The one we just perused
And the result of their prideful knowitallness
Meant the Way of Being and Becoming
Couldn't quite breathe in alignment anymore
Like the Chinese lantern got bent out of shape
And we
Those of us
Still trying to figure out
How our blues and reds and yellows all fit together
Got really confused

Efforts to straighten things out
And portray the whole picture
The blueprint
That helps our minds recognize roses and what their scent is
Were only partial
And we were left with a misshapen twisted
No way Way

Until

Superimpose the figure of a man
Over the whole picture

He came out of the blue
And with his Rose Red
Made their own patch of petals
Peopling their universe
With beings that come in seven different hues
Seven again eh

From the beginning
Our man knew he needed to be
To inhabit every frequency of being in his universe
Even the twisted bits

Especially the twisted bits
Because these were his own kids
Who had messed things up
And even if he couldn't bring them back into the garden
He wanted all the innocent bystanders who'd been caught up in
the mess
To at least have a chance to get the picture for themselves
And get to choose if they wanted to be embraced
In the light of the rose
Or not

To all his trusted helpers he said
Do whatever you can
To make this right
I say this now
Because I have been in and as
All of you
And I know first hand what it is like
What you are going through

So inspirers and guides were filled with blue light
And sent
They came and went
Most in ignominy and pain
Until someone came up with the idea
Of a Book
A Big Blue Book
They can't kill a book
They figured
Especially once it's out on the internet
Three concentric circles on the cover
Expand in three dimensions

One
Up and down

You and me
All in One

Two
Side to side
And all around
Like ripples expanding from the first stone
Like petals

Three
Back to front
Past and future
The breathing light of universes

I tell you this
To give your mind
Which has a bit of blue in it too
A scaffold to work with
To climb on
To work out the twisted kinks
So you can relax
And know
I am with you

He said

Always

Tinkling the Ivories

My spine is a line of time
Tailbone rooted in ancient ooze
Instincts of ancestors rise to unseat me
But crowned I am
Frontal lobes channel divine guidance
And amid endless memories
My monitor sits
Mending my past with threads of the future

Knit one
Pearl one
Knit two together
Knitting and bleating
My Mrs.Utah Watkins
Wages her contented war with entropy
And I, not I AM, but me
I dingle the doorbell of Father Time
Hoping and praying every day
That my goodness is good enough to be great
But more than great
Useful

Deep breath
Sigh
Let go the rope of hope
So high strung it strangles will
Yahoo lasso
Loose the noose from tinkling tips
Slam grooving tootsies
On brilliant xylophonic pads of potential
Flagrantly delicti
Caught in the act of creating
An I

That's you
Ya Hu

Mayhap one drop
From your dancing dervish brow
Will hit the mark

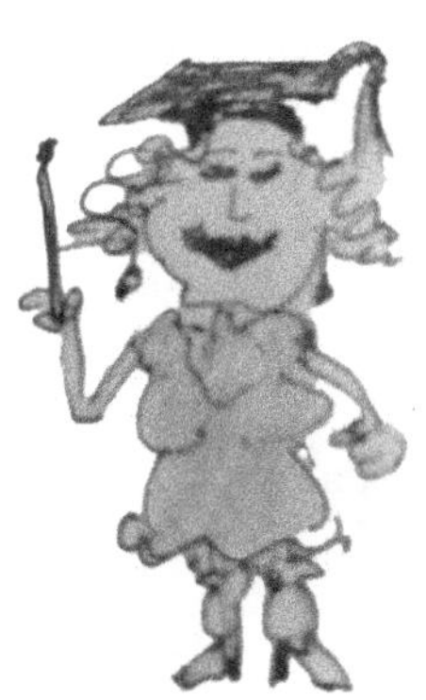

Ever Light

Look up
Look in
Wherever you look
Light

As long as you are able to look
And then beyond
When seeing is more with the soul
The light of life persists
Pulsing away
Even though
Choking darkness
Disappointment and despair
Dim it
Confuse it
And well nigh drown it
Living light shimmers
In stars
In chloroplasts
In skin
Making out of carbon and calcium
Dirt and stone
A thing that lives
And squirms
Smokes dope
And hopes

Light was so dim for so long
We forgot we were part of it
And so came an emissary
An unforgettable reminder
That light is made
Out of the lovemaking
Of Being and Possibility

Like a mighty ancient lighthouse
Built on a slim finger
Pointed into a Mediterranean Sea
Whose carefully tended fire
(How the heck did they get all the wood up there)
Reflects in giant hand polished mirrors
We are illuminated
Guided
Reminded to remember and celebrate
That when all is said and done
We are lighted safely home

I don't have to chase a lightning strike
Or exhaust myself
Creating friction enough
To press smoke into flame
I just flick my bic
And ignite the wick
Of my beeswax candle
In hope
And re-real-ize
That I too am light
And my job
My delight
Is
Shine

For God and Gold

Almost as old as the hills she has lain in
Since the day she first opened her eyes to wisdom
She now strives to wake again
To grasp for the gold ring
Adangle from the sky hook of the gods

So many times in the long ages past
She woke
To find that the prince who must have kissed her
Had high tailed it
Or possibly been kidnapped
Just as he reached for her limp and close to lifeless hand

You'd think it was a conspiracy
That someone didn't want her
To blow the dust from her crown
Actually a marvellous thought amplifying machine in disguise
And wield her sceptre
The one that compels goodness from the hearts of men
With a truth and power all its own
And claim the throne so rightly hers

Jack
A veritably invisible being
Watches her from the window sill
He lifts his head from his fists in anticipation
As she stirs once again

Jack
Short for a name and number
Registered in the annals of time
Not long after Adam and Eve admitted defeat
Yet struggled bravely on
In spite of their pending mortality

Jack
Has pinched and prodded many an aspiring soul
To brave the forest of brambles
To climb the stairs of this ancient tumulus
To step into this chamber where she now lies asleep
And dreaming of a world of children and fruit
Deep rolling waters and dragons
And though they pause to gawp at the sleeping beauty
They barely brush their lips against her mushroom soft cheek
As they bend to peer beneath the bed
Bent only on finding the gold

Ah but Jack
Did not one come
Only a scant millennium or so ago
Who loved her so much
That all the people in her dream
Have grown more human because of it
His kiss still lingers on her lips
And yet she sleeps on

He comes sometimes to join our Jack
Sighing and waiting on the window sill
For a spirit with enough spunk
To kiss her awake
To stop fumbling under her bed
For the gold they will never find

What will happen when she awakens
To see the world in a man's eyes gazing back at her
Will the dream of true love explode into reality
Will light and life suddenly bloom
Will mysteries long embedded in the rock of ages
Pulse ruby red and alive
And connect the Big Heart Of All Things
To her dream

Acknowledgments

My heartfelt thanks to the ongoing support of the Grand Forks Writers Guild and the Urantia community.

This book was made possible by the faithful help of Duane Johnson, Smoky Hills Publishing.

About the Author

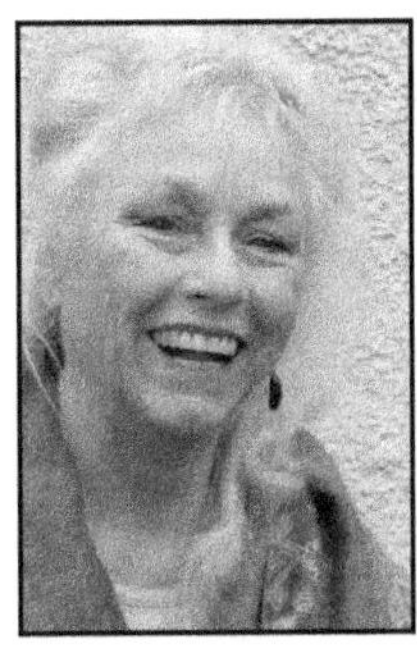

Peri Best lives in a small city in British Columbia, Canada. She began writing at a very early age. Her grade 2 teacher, Miss Short, had her read her poems to the grade 6 class. Music and art, dance and theatre, plus years of practice in the healing art of Energy Kinesiology, all have claimed her time and attention over the years (let's not forget marriages, animals, children and grandchildren thrown in for good measure).

Throughout her life Peri has been a spiritual seeker and finder. Traditional religion, then Sufism and many years of study of *The Urantia Book* have informed much of her thinking. You can find her book, *Belonging—Exploring Healing and Spirituality*, on the web.